Agei…

A So… …

Ghetto-Land

by

Georgina Bray

Assistant Anglican Chaplain, University of Nottingham

GROVE BOOKS LIMITED
Bramcote Nottingham NG9 3DS

CONTENTS

THE COVER PICTURE

is by Greg Forster

ACKNOWLEDGEMENTS

The author and publishers gratefully acknowledge the permission granted by Faber and Faber Ltd. to reproduce the extended quotation from William Golding's *Free Fall* (published by Faber and Faber Ltd., 1961 edn.) in Appendix 1 below.

With happy memories of Carey Heard who first prompted my thinking, and with thanks to Roy McCloughry who guided it in this direction.

First Impression April 1991

ISSN 0951-2667

ISBN 1 85174 175 5

INTRODUCTION

'It makes me wonder if I really do know God after all . . .'

This is the experience of an 80-year-old friend who has been an active church member all her life. She is speaking about her church—what the church now tells her God is like, how she is expected to worship and what she recognizes as her changing position in the community of the church. It is not that her church is uncaring, nor that she is not loved there, but that at the time that she needs help to make sense of her ageing in the light of her faith (and *vice versa*), their attention is elsewhere. The teaching, prayer and pastoral care is geared to young people, new Christians, Christian leaders with busy jobs and growing families . . .

The initial impetus for this study came from a desire to understand the background against which women like this (and hers is a common enough story) come to terms with their own ageing, why they find themselves at the edges at church as well as in society, and what resources the church has to prevent old age becoming 'a sort of ghetto-land' in terms both of the individual lifespan and the position of elderly members in the life of the church.

Although some of the material will be more widely applicable it is intended to address issues relating to normal ageing rather than to specifically pathological ageing, and to those who are able to attend church, whether or not they choose to do so in practice.

The material relates to the current situation in Britain, with the particular tensions and fragmentation our society faces at present, as we come to terms with the limitations of recent trends in economic and social life. This includes the *failure of individualism* (including notions of autonomous 'rights' and private consumer greed) to add up into a successful society, and the *inadequacy of systems* (including the welfare state and management strategies) to create a community in which human beings find identity, meaning and continuity; and the need to establish shared values out of which such communities and traditions can develop. It also includes a *loss of historical perspective,* and thus of the sense of our own place in history, and attempts to regain or replace it by an impotent nostalgia by some, or an anxious utopianism (whether technological or ecological!) by others.

In such a context older people are amongst the primary losers. They are typically regarded as passive recipients of welfare policy and provision (passive clients of a system rather than active members of a community), and as indulging in private reminiscence and nostalgia rather than as a means to valuable continuity and traditions in periods of instability and transition.

In the first two sections we shall consider some of the characteristics of ageing, and how our society operates with regard to old age. Section 3 highlights the place of elderly people in the Christian tradition and Section 4 raises the issue of how we might prepare ahead for our own old age.

The official Church of England report, published after I had done my main work, is the subject of a separate appendix for which I am grateful to Greg Forster.

Georgina Bray
March 1991

1. AGEING

> 'Ageing is a complex sequence of changes. The organs and functions of the body are impaired. Some people suffer mild or severe psychological disorders brought on by degenerative disease or other causes. There are changes in sensory and motor capacities, in the central processing functions associated with intelligence, and in its physical basis—the nervous system. People's position in society changes; their beliefs, attitudes and personal qualities alter, as does their behaviour. The content and organisation of their experience changes . . . These changes lead to greater deterioration, and culminate in death.'[1]

Traditional storytelling has portrayed the ageing process by a variety of images; like sand in an hour-glass, the body contains a fixed quantity of life, which simply trickles away; in a life-long conflict between forces of goodness and healing and forces of destruction and disease, the forces of good are inexorably overcome; like a seed ripening in a shell, life forms and ripens inside a frail body and is renewed upon death.

Those who have aged are characterized as holders of wisdom (for example, the wise wizard without whom the young hero cannot fulfil his mission); as evil and bitter (the wicked witch who deceives little children, but is herself eventually defeated by good); as ridiculous and pitiable (the 'dirty old man', or the amorous old woman despised by Latin satirists); as decrepit ('What I find most lamentable about old age is that one feels one is now repulsive to the young[2]'; or, simply as necessary:

> 'Hobson, do you want anything?'
> 'I want to be younger.'
> 'Sorry. It's your job to be old.'[3]

Generally, a distinction is now made between chronological old age) 'I'm 73') and functional old age ('I can't hurry like I used to'), though in our society compulsory retirement tends to blur the distinction. It may be true that 'you're only as old as you feel', but for the most part stereotyping sets a pattern of ageing to which people are expected to conform from retirement onwards. Poor health, conservatism and inflexibility, mental decline, unhappiness, loneliness, dependence and uselessness as necessarily the case in old age are myths[4], but are perpetuated in ageing as we learn to expect and then to conform to them.

Although most people live to experience old age, it is by no means a uniform experience, with variations from individual to individual, and between class, gender and race; and 'the elderly' are not a uniform group, as they span as much as forty years in our culture. Nevertheless, ageing is inevitably characterized by a number of losses:

[1] Bromley, *The Psychology of Human Ageing,* p.15.
[21] Caecilius, quoted in de Beauvoir, *Old Age,* p.134.
[3] Dudley Moore and John Gielgud in the film *Arthur*.
[4] Scrutton, *Counselling Older People,* pp.15f.

Physical and mental decline: stereotypical attitudes to health and ability in old age exaggerate the expectations of decline ('Well, what can you expect at your age?'), and assume that symptoms are due more to medical than environmental factors than is necessarily the case (for example, hypothermia, greater incidence of illness in retired manual than managerial workers, urinary incontinence linked to social fears). Nevertheless, certain biological decline is an inevitable part of the natural process of ageing. Some cells cease to replace themselves (e.g. muscle cells, resulting in loss of strength without exercise); skin becomes thinner and blood vessels smaller (easier bruising and longer recovery time); the cells of the nervous system do not reproduce (malajusted balance, poor maintenance of body temperature and blood pressure, the memory losses); sense of smell, taste and hearing decline. A general increase in frailty, and a gradual 'loss of enjoyable functioning'[1] is characteristic of ageing, with greater or lesser effect on psychological wellbeing and lifestyle.

Retirement: Retirement from employment can itself be a compound of losses—loss of activity and routine, changing financial status, loss of companionship and membership of a working community, loss of status and loss of interests outside the home/family life. In a culture where retired people have no defined role, retirement ceremonies must be adequate to function as 'rites of passage' through these losses, or they will signal only an end and not also a beginning. As well as retirement from employment there are successive withdrawals from other social activities and responsibilities, either because of social pressure to make way for younger people, or because of illness or frailty. This compounds the losses of retirement from employment, particularly of role and status.

Finance: loss of income after retirement particularly affects manual workers, though even averaged figures in 1987 showed that elderly families in Britain received only 67% of the population's averaged income (compared to an averaged 82% in Canada, Germany, Israel, Norway, Sweden and USA)[2], and in 1981 more than half the retired people in Britain were living below the official poverty line.[3] In 1986 a Family Expenditure Survey indicated that the normal weekly disposable income of men aged 65+, living alone and dependent mainly on state pensions (over two-thirds of the sample) was £78.62 compared to £133.55 for men under 65.[4] Diminished financial status demands an altered lifestyle, and increasing loss of social activities.

Bereavement: the loss through death both of primary relationships and of a general social network becomes increasingly marked, and as well as causing loneliness and isolation for some, increases the awareness of our own mortality.

Dependency-reversal: for those with children the loss of the parental role occurs in stages through the child's adolescence and young adulthood, but a gradual (or, for some, sudden) reversal of dependence (or completion of a 'cycle of dependence') occurs finally during ageing.

[1] Rayner, *Human Development*, p.256.
[2] Hedstrom and Ringen, cited in Burton, *Old Age Phobia*, p.12.
[3] Bornat, Phillipson and Ward, cited in Burton, *op. cit.*, p.13.
[4] Dept. of Employment Family Expenditure Survey 1986.

Although these losses are unavoidable in ageing there is no reason to consider them less traumatic than at other stages of life, particularly as they occur together in a short period of time. They may, however, have different meanings in old age; for example, death of peers may seem less tragic in old age but signals a declining circle of friends with shared memories and fewer opportunities to continue widening the circle.

However, as well as being a time of losses, old age is also characterized by the accumulated experiences of a lifetime, which if positive give a sense of security and identity through the losses, or add to feelings of despair if negative. How we cope with the losses of ageing depends largely on how we have responded to experiences throughout life and what we become as a result. Old age provides the opportunity for 'life-review'—to revise the lifecycle and integrate the external events and the internal self, and to find ways of coping with ageing. During this process personality traits which have been partly submerged during earlier life (by social convention, activity, the needs of others etc.) become more evident—we become more clearly what we *are*.

How we accept our own ageing is fundamentally influenced by the attitudes of those around us, and the value which the wider culture in which we live gives to elderly people. We will examine this in the next section, focussing on those features in our society which contribute to distorted views of old people, and to ageism.

2. AGEING IN SOCIETY

Britain, like other Western, urban-industrial countries, is an 'ageing society' with an increasing proportion of the total population being both 'young-old' (65-74) and 'old-old' (75+). At present, one in every five of the population is aged 60+.[1] The proportion of elderly aged 65-74 is declining and will continue to do so during the next decade (second World War casualties and post-war emigration), so that by the end of the century the very elderly will constitute 45% of the total elderly.[2] Hygiene and medical advances continue to increase life expectancy, so that the expected number of years beyond retirement is increasing. However, despite their large presence in British society, elderly people have a low profile. Like other groups without wealth, power or a recognized economic role, they are, typically, the victims of an '-ism'. But unlike racism or sexism, ageism is an oddly self-destructive prejudice, because we are all potentially the victim.

Like other prejudices, ageism works as a combination of passive and active factors, which accumulate implicitly to exclude or denigrate or make invisible older people.

On one hand prejudices by work EXCLUSION. Even a fragmented society develops certain values, and a dominant self-image in accordance with those values. Members of the society who do not fit the image find themselves ignored and excluded and drift to the margins, so the values and image are not challenged and altered:

Patterns of progress and change. In pre-technological, agricultural society, the passage of time is cyclical. Inherent in the cycle is a continuity between the past and the future: seed is planted and harvested and replanted; the oral tradition of the elders passes on experience and wisdom and identity to those who follow them, who in turn become wise for their descendants. In post-agricultural society, this cyclical view of time and community is replaced by a linear view in which achievement is not measured in terms of successful completion of a cycle, but of forward movement away from the primitive past to a bright, progressive future: 'Every day in every way we're getting better and better . . .'.

In technological society, up-to-the-minute knowledge is more valuable than accrued wisdom, and knowledge very quickly becomes out of date. The present needs to be severed from an unfashionable past, and those whose knowledge is thought to represent that past do not themselves have a place in the new society. Although it is a normal part of ageing to hand on responsibilities to younger men and women, ageism is unable to recognize that those who are now old were once young, and that those who are now young will be the old people in the future of the society. 'Old' and 'young' are externalized as static categories of people and become synonyms for 'past' (bad) and 'present/future' (good). Old people are not regarded as 'our future selves', and so can be safely marginalized to give precedence to younger people.

[1] Cited in BBC2 documentary as above.
[2] Cited in Phillipson, *Capitalism and the Construction of Old Age,* p.8.

Production and consumption. In a technological and capitalist (and media-mad) society, a primary means of valuing people is in terms of what they produce—in particular their employment, but also their use of leaisure time and their family; and what they consume—material wellbeing as an indicator of personal value. But national retirement policy makes many men and women over 60/65 artificially dependent on the state or their savings, and decreases their ability to consume by removing their ability to produce. At worst, there is a tacit assumption that the elderly are burdensome consumers who do not 'deserve' to consume because they no longer produce (regardless of their previous productivity, and unlike the very young whose consumption now is acceptable because they will produce later).

Individualism. Our society is highly individualistic; Lasch suggests that it is the 'cult of self' rather than the 'cult of youth' which is at the heart of ageism.[1] Independence and control over our circumstances are highly prized rights; competition and individual success (defined by strict social copnvention) mark out the strong; the 'inner self' is a focus for improvement and fulfilment and the justification for attitudes and actions ('if it feels right, it is right'). Society should be more that the sum total of individuals, but extreme individualism weakens links between people, and between generations. 'Shared meanings' in a community are superceded by individual meanings, which fail to form a corporate identity or tradition to pass between generations, and weaken the community role of older people. And some of the processes of ageing itself threaten personal autonomy when the result in dependence on others, and so are a sort of personal 'scandal'.

Death. As medicine and hygiene have improved, death has become a less common occurrence through the lifecycle, and proportionately more common in old age. A widespread health service makes death more common in hospital than at home, and undertakers and clergy and other experts take care of the final practicalities. Death has become altogether less public, and British reserve and custom keep grief private. It is possible in life both to ignore death, and to fear it as an outrage against independence and self-control, and under the influence of secularism to regard it as the end of the self. In our society the tendency is to draw back from anything from which we might 'catch' death or which reminds us of our own mortality (compare attitudes to cancer or HIV/AIDS). The elderly, more obviously (though not necessarily actually) closer to death, can be an unwelcome reminder of mortality, and so are kept aside.

Prejudices also work by DISTORTION, by a combination of **levelling** and **sharpening**. The differences between old people are levelled so that they all appear more similar, and the differences between old people and 'everybody else' are sharpened so that they appear to form a distinct and separate group:

Uniformity. There is an assumption that by virtue of chronological age old people are a homogeneous group. Once over 65 their interests and needs become the same (though different from those of the rest of the population!). Class, gender, race, personal history, and an age range of as much as thirty years are ignored, and they are regarded, and treated, *en masse*.

[1] Lasch, *The Culture of Narcissism*, p.217.

Inevitability. There is an assumption that stereotypical conditions of ageing are inevitable: that old people, by definition, suffer ill-health, mental deterioration, isolation and unhappiness; that old people, by definition, become inflexible, conservative and awkward . . . These effects are seen as natural symptoms of ageing, not of disease or social or environmental factors. This maintains a generation gap: 'they' are ill and inflexible because they are old; 'we' are not ill or inflexible, therefore we are not ageing.

Simplicity. This is the 'all you need, dear . . .' approach! The difficulties encountered in ageing are not as real as in other age groups, and are easy to deal with: a helping hand, a listening ear will restore tranquillity. The elderly have regressed to a second childhood and can be treated as children.

Ageism is damaging in so far as it restricts old people, who learn to 'live down' to its expectations. The ideologies and social structures that maintain ageism go unchallenged, and the stereotypes become self-fulfilling as every generation takes the attitudes they held about the elderly in their youth, and internalizes them as they themselves grow old.

Although **society's** response to ageing is one of exclusion and distortion, this response is not entirely absent from the **church**. Stereotypical assumptions about conservatism and tradition, high value placed on new expressions of worship rather than on accumulated wisdom, and a predominance of youth-centred activities and resources all contribute to an increasingly peripheral place in the church's life for people as they age. However, rather than focussing on the manifestations of ageism in church, in the next section we shall shift the emphasis from us/them attitudes to our corporate participation in the resources of a tradition which embraces all ages.

3. THE CHRISTIAN TRADITION AND AGEING

The Christian tradition has a variety of resources with which to give meaning to living even in the face of ageing. In this section we shall consider a selection of these resources—biblical, thematic and pastoral—and the light they shed on ageing; not as special, separate resources for the elderly, or even as a special application for the elderly, but as elements of a shared heritage which naturally includes elderly people. We shall avoid expressions like 'the ethical task' and other forms of us/them language that imply that 'we' (the younger ones who are now at the centre of things) have the resources to help 'you' (who have aged and are therefore at the edge of things).

Although this section does not include a check-list for church action, such lists are readily available elsewhere (see for example *Life Later On* by Ann Webber for some useful hints). It is obviously important that church **practice** (including facilities, worship and other events) reflects and promotes an ethos in which all ages belong equally in the community of faith.

The meaning of life in old age. In looking optimistically at living in the face of ageing, we must ensure an appropriate and realistic meaning of 'living' in old age without, for example, overcompensating against stereotypes of passivity, conservatism etc., to expect 'activity' and 'growth' in terms more appropriate to other stages of life.

(i) Old age is a part—a full part—of life. Knierim writes:

> 'Ageing and old age are not periods of transition between life and death, and not at all the first phase of death. They belong to life . . . and however burdensome life may be, it is still life vis-à-vis death.'[1]

Clearly, it is more difficult in some experiences of ageing than in others to see old age as fully life and not 'this sort of ghetto-land tacked on at the end', but we are compelled to search for meaning and give value in even the most distressing appearances of ageing. A woman working with psycho-geriatric patients recalled the prayer of one, 'Lord, let me see this time as an honour, not as a ludicrous mistake'. In a beauty- and youth-dominated culture, in church as well as in society. this requires a particular love for and attentiveness to the individual.

(ii) Models of human development through the lifecycle (despite their dangers[2]) help to emphasize maturity rather than mid-adulthood as the goal, and suggest that maturity has different meanings for different stages of life. Common to the theories of, for example, Jung, Erikson, Kohlberg and Fowler are two interrelating themes, drawing together the experiences of life and acclimatizing to death through personal and social integration:

—personal integration: after the phase of productivity:

'establishing oneself' (which Jung places only up to c40 years), activity, is a period of bringing together all the experiences of life and parts

[1] Knierim, in Clements (ed.), *Ministry and the Construction of Old Age,* pp. 22, 24.

[2] That they imply uniformity of development from person to person, or are followed slavishly as standards of maturity and personal achievement.

of the self to find a unity in them, and to accept what we become in a lifetime.

—social integration (or 'cosmic perspective'![1]):
a growing awareness and acceptance of our place 'in the whole', and with the resultant decline in fears of 'threats to the self' an easing of the defensive urgency of self-preservation.

The models of development show the lifecycle as a natural progression from birth to death, and not as a graph which peaks in early middle-age and thereafter declines; and encourage healthy living through ageing rather than 'fending off' decline for as long as possible.

(iii) Throughout life, 'successful' living must embrace the whole person—body, mind and spirit—as part of social units as well as as an individual. There are strong pressures against this view in old age. Faced with physical and mental decline spiritual activity is over-emphasized in old age, assuming for example that old people become a power-house of prayer in the church as they become increasingly inactive. Keyes compares expectations and reality of prayer in 'the second half of life'[2], suggesting that while expectations are that prayer supercedes activity and guards against loneliness, in reality ageing brings new difficulties to praying, and that expectations are self-serving projections placed on the elderly by those who feel they are too busy to pray themselves. Some older people are less at ease with their faith as they find church practice changing around them, and find faith harder to express if the familiar traditions and language are no longer available to them.

(iv) Disengagement theories[3] have suggested that people positively welcome the isolation that increasing age can bring. Although isolation does not necessarily mean desolation, the suggestion is hard to accept, both because of the scale of the isolation (for example, a survey in 1978 found that 29% women aged 75-84 lived alone and that 44% of those had done so for more than 20 years[4]) and because of its causes—very often bereavements in primary relationships, family mobility, and enforced (through social convention, illnesses etc.(withdrawal from social activities and responsibilities. At every stage in life we form and maintain identity in relation to others and as body, mind and soul, and this must be interpreted sensitively and appropriately in old age.

BIBLICAL RESOURCES

This section highlights material explicitly concerning old age, though there is always a danger in seeking out the experiences of old people recorded in the Bible and appropriating them too simplistically in pastoral encounters. (An example of such misappropriation might be to use God's

[1] The term is Jacobs', in a description of Kohlberg's Stage 7, *Towards the Fullness of Christ,* p.43.

[2] In Davies (ed.), *Studies in Pastoral Theology and Social Anthropology,* pp.82ff.

[3] Disengagement theories were pioneered in the 1950s by Cummings and Henry, suggesting that the elderly withdraw from the world to prepare for death; the theories are currently unpopular, being regarded as justifying social structures which cause elderly people to withdraw whether or not they wish to do so.

[4] Cited in Phillipson, *op. cit.,* p.72.

call to Abraham as a model to urge activity and a clinging to life, when what is needed is a sharing in the recognition of the nearness of death:

> 'I don't have much longer to go now.'
> 'Nonsense, you've years ahead of you. Look at Abraham, he was 75 when God called him. You never know what God's got lined up for you.')

So, this is not a collection of 'proof-texts' into which old people can be neatly fitted, but pointers towards attitudes to ageing and old age appropriate to the community of God's people.

Old age as integral to the lifespan:

* Writers are quite realistic about the distressing symptoms of old age. Barzillai's declinging discernment, taste and hearing are recorded (2 Sam. 19.35), and 'the Preacher' graphically describes similar losses of sight, teeth, physical strength . . . (Eccl. 12.2ff); our span of years 'is but trouble and sorrow' (Ps. 90.10).

* Nevertheless, old age—fullness of years—is seen as a blessing from God within the covenant relationship. 'Grey hair is a crown of splendour; it is attained by a righteous life' (Prov. 16.31), 'He will renew your life and sustain you in your old age' (Ruth 4.15), and, symbolically, in the exaggerated lifespans of the patriarchs.

Old age and its symptoms need not be denied or be felt to be a source of shame; it is a natural part of the lifespan, and a time in which God may be found as much as at any other time.

Old age as integral to society

* Elihu makes it clear that not *only* the old are wise (Job 32.6ff), but there is a theme of wisdom in old age, bringing corporate tradition to life for the present generation—'Remember the days of old, consider the generations long past. Ask your father and he will tell you, your elders and they will explain to you.' (Deut. 32.7). Israel's identity is rooted in memory, and the elderly have a special role in maintaining the nation's faith by recalling God's activity in the past.

* Respect for the elderly is a mark of a well-ordered society. Provision is made for widows in Israelite law and early church order, and at the heart of the law the command is given to adults to honour their parents. Disrespect for the elderly is a sign of chaos in society—'The young will rise up against the old' is a judgment on Hudah and Jerusalem (Is. 3.5), and there is threat of attack by a 'fierce-looking nation without respect for the old' for a disobedient Israel (Deut. 28.50).

* The elderly are visible throughout the passage of 'salvation-history'—the patriarchs as the epitome of wisdom in age; the story of Ruth from the perspective of Naomi, finding the faithful kindness of God even in the bitterness of loss and age; Simeon and Anna greeting and proclaim

ing the Saviour (Luke 2); the promise of the Spirit to old as well as young (Joel 2), and of a full age in the New Heaven and Earth (Is. 65.20).

Elderly people are not 'yesterday's church', just as young people are not 'tomorrow's church'. They are integral to the community of faith (and to God's creation in the world) at every time.

THEMATIC RESOURCES

Vocation. Under the influence of Luther and Calvin the notion of vocation came to mean the duties and lifestyle through which faith was expressed, rather than the call to belief itself. Although this helps to emphasize that faith is to be lived out in a whole lifestyle and not just in religious activities, it tends to be an 'activist' view—we serve God by 'doing things'. The original New Testament meaning of vocation is clearer for those who are very passive—who 'do' nothing through which to fulfill such a vocation, or for those letting go of activities in retirement. Our vocation is a calling into the Kingdom of God (1 Thess. 2.12), and therefore to fellowship (1 Cor. 1.9), to peace (Col. 3.15), to hope (Eph. 1.18) ... Acceptance of the call is marked by baptism, a lifelong sign and seal of new life. There is no retirement from this vocation, and it is not measured by our 'usefulness' or degree of activity, but is lived out in responsiveness to God (and so to our neighbour) within our particular capabilities and circumstances.

Hope. The Christian tradition has much to say about the nature of hope, particularly in relation to identity, to give confidence through all the changes in a single life; and especially so when frailty and the death of peers are a reminder of mortality.

* God's covenant with us is a secure one: 'God is for us' and 'nothing in all creation will be able to separate us from the love of God in Christ Jesus' (Rom. 8), including death or whatever decline precedes it.

* Our future has continuity with our past: all the experiences and pleasures that have made us 'us' carry us into our future. We do not know *how* we shall be in the future (either side of death) but we do know that our essential self—the 'real me'—is what continues. It is this 'real me' that is created by and relates to God, and this relationship will not be destroyed.

* As well as this, however, the Christian tradition of hope includes an element of *dis*continuity with the past, in a different sense. Continuity with the past refers to the certain hope of personal identity continuing; discontinuity with the past concerns the real possibility of redemption, in its widest sense. We are not restricted to what we have been: real change is possible so that we are not limited by what has happened to us so far. Our identity can be more than simply the addition of all that's happened to us; we shall be given a 'new name'. We anticipate and experience this future hope in the present; our dying and rising with Christ in faith (and all the little deaths and rebirths of a life of faith) give us a foretaste of a quite different dying and rising that is promised for our future resurrection.

The image of God and the Incarnation: being 'like God'. Human beings are created in the image of God (Gen. 1.26). Men and women, black and white, disabled and able-bodied, young and old equally participate in the likeness of God and reflect that likeness by being fully, freely human. It may be that our assumptions about God lead us to make assumptions about what state of humanity most accurately reveals the image of God (and who is more 'spiritual' because of it), but the truth is that for all of us it is our most essential humanity that is made in God's likeness and which is taken up by Jesus in the Incarnation. What makes *us* 'like God' in this sense, is not that we approximate to the externals of whatever stereotype we have of God (male, powerful, active etc.), but that our humanness, created and affirmed by God, is taken up and redeemed by Christ in the Incarnation; and that it is given back to us so that it can be lived in a particular form (white, young, female, etc.) without being hampered by the stereotypes and prejudices and obligations that usually go with that form, so that we are liberated to become more and more as God intended.

Having seen in Jesus the possibilities of a human life lived to the fullest extent for God's glory, we look to him for glimpses of what our own human life might be like. This means looking beneath the incidentals (Jesus was young, male, etc.) to the presence of God in basic human experiences. For example, Jesus knew loss of status,, vulnerable dependence on others, insecurity in earthly terms, and suffering in death within the scope of God's love. If these are our experiences in getting old (or at any age) the good news is not that they are magically removed by God, but that they may be radically redefined in God's presence, according to Jesus' own experience. Security and status based on material wellbeing can be replaced by security in wellbeing of relationships (with God, neighbour and self). And relationship is no longer about competition, independence or selfish pleasure, but about interdependence where vulnerability has as much place as strength. And the place of suffering is given form by the crucifixion which shows the potential of a way of living which includes and transforms pain.

Weakness and equality. Whatever definition society gives to 'value' (and our own society defines it largely in terms of power and productivity and innovation), at the heart of the Christian gospel is God's 'kenosis'—self-emptying to a point of extraordinary vulnerability, becoming weak rather than grasping hold of strength, and by so doing redefining terms and allocating weakness a new place in the order of 'acceptability'. Or rather, not a new place, but underlining the place it had throughout Israel's history, from the formulating of the law onwards (e.g. Lev. 19.9, just harvesting for the poor and the stranger). The weak or poor do not have special privileges, special value, by virtue of their weakness, nor are they to be included into the scheme of things by special charity; by right they have equal place, are equally valued. And when that right is not fulfilled and they are absent or marginal then the whole society suffers the loss. Older people are not a uniformly powerless group (though the stereotype may be more true than not), but to the extent that some elderly individuals are powerless, with regard to either personal circumstances or position in society, then our attitude should reflect that of the 'humble, kenotic

Christian God (who) will not intervene, but co-creates only as we allow or invite. Such a God infuses, supports and enhances our life, without making us objects.'[1] In such a community those who are weak do not need to use their weakness to manipulate the strong, and those who are strong will neither patronize nor exclude the weak. Equality in the Christian faith is not only a matter of equality between individuals, but of equality of membership of the community of faith, which finds expression in fellowship. Every member has a part in the Body of Christ, and if one part is absent all suffer. As we age we are not incorporated by the charity of younger members, but by our own standing in Christ are inextricably part of the whole.

PASTORAL RESOURCES

In this final section of resources we shall consider three themes of pastoral care that seem particularly relevant in the experience of ageing. Although the language of pastoral care tends towards 'carer' and 'cared for' mutuality based on common humanity must lie behind our ethic of care for one another.

Presence. Much of our knowledge of ourselves and of God is formed and maintained through our lifetime in relationships, but as the social circle declines in old age there are fewer relationships in which to test our identity and through which to find God's love. Although to be 'simply present' may seem inadequate, less effective that 'doing', at best it provides a relationship in which God's care and attention are expressed. Campbell writes of this, 'Can we bring a presence to . . . people which communicates the being of a loving and utterly trustworthy God?'.[2] Of course, this is not a technique which can be measured for success, but stems from a responsiveness to God's regard for the individual, and a sense of the overall purpose of care and needs in ageing that gives meaning to each encounter as part of a larger whole. Our presence can not only reveal but respond to God in the relationship. To communicate, 'I find God here with you' can assure the elderly of their 'Christlikeness' and stimulate their faith, and affirm their home as a place where God is present. Our willingness to be in another's home, their 'world', which is often a means of self-expression in our culture, expresses an ease to be with them and an acceptance of who they are. Moving at their pace, living briefly on their terms, puts their way of life at the centre—makes it the norm for another as well as for them—and so affirms its value. To receive hospitality (though not to demand or presume it), however simply, shares in the order of another's life, and reassures that they have control over their day-to-day events.

Presence is, necessarily physical. With great sensitivity, 'bodily caring'[3] can affirm the body: eye contact, touch, even tea-and-biscuits, can provide an ordinary physical acceptance from which to support the more difficult tasks of re-evaluating self-image and overcoming shame or dislike, to take into account a declining and sometimes uncontrollable body.

[1] Maggie Ross, *Pillars of Flame* (SCM, London, undated) p.14.
[2] Campbell, *Paid to Care,* p.102.
[3] Campbell, *op. cit.,* p.102.

Listening. Active, emphatic listening forms a central part of all pastoral care, and especially as we come to terms with ageing. Models of development referred to above indicate the need to find completeness, unity within ourself and *vis-à-vis* the world, and it seems that reminiscence is a key to this. An extended quote from Golding's *Free Fall* is included as an appendix, to illustrate the longing to make sense of ourselves, to find 'a pattern which fits over everything'. Telling our story—sometimes over and over again!—seems to have several purposes in ageing. Positively, it 'maintains a storyline'[1], reassuring us of the continuity of 'me' throughout our life, in the light of what has gone before; it brings to the surface 'unfinished business (regrets, unfulfilled ambitions, bitterness) and invites resolution or acceptance; and it finds a hope for the future from the familiar echoes of the past. Negatively, it can be an escape from the unpleasant present into what is perceived as a safer past.

Randall[2] suggests three ways of listening that care in the tasks of story-telling in ageing:

(i) by simple listening, with empathy and appreciation, to the whole story, we can communicate that the story, and the *person*, is really heard. Sometimes stories are told so often that they take on a set-form (which may or may not be factually accurate) as a sort of personal 'creed' of identity and self-perception, which can be unlocked and shared by sympathetic listening.

(ii) by prompting story-telling, and revealing conncections between fragments of a story or between different stories, we can help the story teller see the meaning behind their stories and find the threads of continuity they seek.

(iii) by reinterpreting the meaning of stories, for example from the perspective of someone else, we can help the story-teller explore new meaning and resolve old conflicts.

Often a story that appears to be only about the past has bearing on the present. Sensitivity to why *this* story is being told *now* can provide clues to current morale or preoccupations, and the means of bringing the story teller more fully into the present with those feelings, rather than remaining with them as memories in the past. Many stories will have shared meanings for the teller and the listener—shared relationships, faith, culture, history. Welcoming these meanings can open the way to a deeper relationship, and they can provide a tacit contract, a code, by which deeper matters are referred to.

Corporate worship. In worship we reach towards God who is 'greater than ourselves', and in our searching we both know ourselves better and we learn to lose ourselves. Our worship expresses our identity but also forms it. And whether we worship with others or alone, our worship unites us in fellowship. For many elderly people, shared worship in their home (sick communion or informal prayer, for example) will be a valuable

[1] Randall, *Reminiscing in the Elderly,* p.211.
[2] Randall, *op. cit.,* pp.212ff.

extension of, or substitute for, congregational worship, but the needs of old people in the congregation must also be respected. *Change* is important if the church is to keep relevant to contemporary concerns, but its form must take account of *all* who are affected by it and not just the most progressive. Rituals, symbols and language point to deeper meanings of belonging, of security and order, and of identity of God and self. They provide a 'touchstone' of certainty and familiarity when much else is uncertain, and form an understood 'meeting place' between people which can be accepted without articulation. When they are changed the meanings behind them can be threatened, and it feels not that the externals have changed, but that we or God have changed. Some elderly members at a church that changed to a nave altar, for example, knew that only the building had changed but felt that God was different: was no longer in the same place, was not so holy, could not be met in the same way; for a few this was liberating, for others very disturbing and alienating (it also marked the preferences of younger church members as more important). So, in initiating change in church we must be aware of what lies behind the traditions and sensitively address those concerns, helping to re-root them in the emerging practices or to find new symbols to address them.

There is, too, a place for both 'integration' and 'segregation' as normals ways of belonging in church life. On one hand, 'all-age' worship (which like 'family' worship seems too often to be a euphemism for children-centred worship!) must include the needs and joys of older people in prayer, in preaching, in blessing (as well as in all the practicalities like hearing facilities). On the other hand, the occasions when older people are separated either intentionally (e.g. Ladies' Fellowships) or unintentionally (8 a.m. communion?!) must be recognized as full parts of the church's life, and not considered peripheral to the main thrust of activities, and given as full and creative support as every other service and activity.

4. CONCLUSION: 'PRACTISING FOR OUR OLD AGE . . .'

Our attitudes to old people and our attitudes to our own ageing are inextricably linked. To regard being old as being 'a problem' is to see old people as a static group to which we do not belong. In order to stay exempt we must deny our own ageing, creating a barrier between our present self and our future self, and isolating ourselves from those whose age reminds us of that future. Conversely, to be at ease with those who have aged is to accept old age as a natural part of the lifecycle, however difficult its manifestations, and to admit it as our own likely fate.

Old age is integral to life. Although awareness of mortality may be heightened, old age is not a withdrawal from life and the world to prepare for death; the concern continues to be with living, albeit with its particular meanings in the face of ageing. And what we make of this living depends on how we have lived throughout our life.

As indicated above, a common theme in development theories of ageing is the need to find a two-fold integration: unity in our self, and unity with the wider world that involves letting go of our self. Although the task of finding this integration may be in some sense 'new' during ageing, it does also build on what has gone before. If we are to prepare ahead for our ageing, we must develop the ability to find echoes of this integration throughout life: living without pretence, true to ourselves and finding value in who we *are* as well as in what we *do*, and accepting our place in a world wider than our own perspective.

This means that throughout life there will be a recognition that 'this is only a stage on the journey'—this is not the goal, but a signpost on the way; things are somewhat tenuous, there are many 'little deaths', choices which involve renunciations, and an acceptance of things not completed. We are 'strangers and pilgrims'. At the same time there will also be a commitment to live wholeheartedly with the present reality, a 'sacrament of the present moment' and gratitude for what *is*; although the signposts point to something as yet unseen, they are a sure continuity between the present and the future, and indicate that even the present has 'eternal significance'.

These two ways of living are intertwined—living wholeheartedly and honestly in the present, true to whatever it consists of, *and* holding to it loosely, loving without possessing, receiving without being manipulative, influencing without grasping power.

This may be a way of 'practising for old age'. As well, it is inherent in the development of a society in which individuals are valued and drawn beyond themselves into a community; and it is the balance of commitment and freedom essential to pastoral care. Perhaps this is because it is a reflection of the painful, hopeful 'now and not yet' of the Kingdom of God in which all our living and ageing takes place.

APPENDIX I

'My yesterdays walk with me. They keep step, they are grey faces that peer over my shoulder . . .

'I must go back and tell the story over. It is a curious story, not so much in the external events which are common enough, but in the way it presents itself to me, the only teller. For time is not to be laid out endlessly like a row of bricks. That straight line from the first hiccup to the last gasp is a dead thing. Time is two modes. The one is an effortless perception native to us as water to a mackerel. The other is a memory, a sense of shuffle fold and coil, of that day nearer than that because more important, of that event mirroring this, or those three set apart, exceptional and out of the straight line altogether . . . I have lived enough of my life to require a pattern that fits over everything I know; and where shall I find that?

'I want to understand. The grey faces peer over my shoulder. Nothing can expunge or exorcize them. The mind cannot hold more than so much; but understanding requires a sweep that takes in the whole of remembered time and then can pause. Perhaps if I write my story as it appears to me I shall be able to go back and select . . .

'To communicate is our passion and our despair.

'I can remember myself as I was when I was a child. But even if I had committed murder then, I should no longer feel responsible for it. There is a threshold here, too, beyond which what we did was done by someone else. Yet I was there. Perhaps, to understand must include pictures from those early days also. Perhaps reading my story through again I shall see the connection between the little boy, clear as spring water, and the man like a stagnant pool. Somehow, the one became the other.'

From William Golding *Free Fall,* ch. 1 (Faber and Faber, London, 1961)

APPENDIX II

The Board for Social Responsibility Report

In 1990 a report of the Church of England's Board for Social Responsibility, entitled simply *Ageing*, was published.[1] Since this present booklet was written originally during 1989 there is no direct reference to the BSR book in the text, though there is considerable overlap in concern. The BSR report contains much sociological information, and information on social policy and current practice in social and health services in the light of recent changes in the welfare state.

Thus, a great deal of what it says bears upon social ethics. There is relatively little (pp.50, 51) on personal ethics, though the key point made is worth repeating; '. . . ethics are centrally relevant to how people age. At the level of personal ethics, the degree to which people experience friendship, loyalty, love, treachery, violence, insensitivity, for example, will enhance or diminish their lives.' One might add that it is in the choices individuals make, in giving as well as responding to these experiences in younger life—practising for old age—that their ageing is shaped. It seems surprising, however, to an evangelical at least, that the report's authors see eucharistic worship (and thanksgiving) as a talisman which will engender a correct approach to ageing. Perhaps they make the age-old ethical confusion between 'is' and 'ought'. Even specific and conscious Christian teaching on the value of repentance, forgiveness and gratitude are all too easily swamped by secular presumptions.

The report shares the concern of this Study, that neither church not society should allow 'ageism' to shape its attitudes to older people.[2] As one might expect, perhaps, in an official report, the criticism is less trenchant, and the portrayal of the ghetto of old age less stark, than here.

While the report recognizes that there may be difficulties for old people in maintaining and expressing their faith, it places greater confidence than this booklet in the use of prayer and spirituality as a remedy for the loneliness and disorientation that old age can bring.[3]

In commenting on the social ethics of ageing, and the treatment of the old, the BSR report again follows the style of an official report, highlighting issues rather than championing a particular policy. It does stress[4] the continued need for public provision (both local and national) for the care of the elderly, despite the rise of the private sector over recent years, and despite the growing emphasis (right in the proper setting) on individual responsibility. Emphasis on the value of the individual should enhance, not diminish, society's sense of responsibility for its weaker members.

G. S. Forster (Series Convenor) April 1991

[1] Church House Publishing, London, 151pp. pb., 95. Linked to this report was a study guide, *Happy Birthday, Anyway!* (CHP 1990) 29pp., £1. 25.
[2] Cf. pp.55-58, 125-127.
[3] Cf. pp.118-122, p.48.
[4] e.g. p.108 §9.39, and the Conclusion §9.61 p.113.

BIBLIOGRAPHY

de Beauvoir s., *Old Age* (Penguin, London, 1972).

Becker, A., 'Pastoral Theoolgical Implications of the Ageing process' in *Journal of Religion and Ageing* Vol. 2:3 (1986) USA.

Board of Social Responsibility, *Ageing* (Church House Publishing, 1900).

Bromley D., *The Psychology of Human Ageing* (Penguin, Harmondsworth, 1974 edit).

Burton, J., *Old Age Phobia* (Jubilee Centre, Cambridge, 1989).

Campbell, A., *Paid to Care* (SPCK, London, 1985).

Clements, W. (ed.), *Ministry with the Ageing* (Harper and Row, San Francisco, 1981).

Clements, W., 'Ageing and the Dimensions of Spiritul Development' in *Journal of Religion and Ageing* Vol. 2.1, 2 (1985/6) USA.

Deeds, D., *Pastoral Theology: An Enquiry* (Epworth, Lonbdon, 1987).

Fowler, J., *Stages of Faith* (Harper and Row, San francisco, 1981).

Halsey, A., *Changes in British Society* Chs. 1, 5 (OUP 1986, edit.).

Jacobs, M., *Towards the Fullness of Christ* (DLT, London, 1988(.

Keyes, G., 'Prayer in the second half of life' in Davies D. (ed.) *Studies in Pastoral Theology and Social Anthropology* (Birmingham University Press, 1986).

Kubler-Ross, E., *Questions and Answers on Death and Dying* (MacMillan, New York, 1974).

Lasch, C., *The Culture of Narcissism* (Norton and Co., New Yor, 1978).

Lessing, D., *The Diaries of Jane Somers* (Penguin, London, 1985).

Lyon, K. B. *Toward a Practical Theology of Aging* (Fortress Press, Philadelphia, 1985).

Nouwen, H., *Ageing—the Fulfillment of Life* (Image, New York, 1976).

Randall, R., 'Reminiscing in the Elderly: Pastoral Care of Self-Narratives' in *Journal of Pastoral Care* (1986) XL.3.

Rayner, E., *Human Development* ch. 15 (Allen and Unwin, London, 1978).

Phillipson, C., *Capitalism and the Construction of Old Age* (MacMillan, London/ Basingstoke, 1982).

Scrutton, S., *Counselling Older People* (Arnold/Age Concern, London, 1989).

Skeet, M., *The Third Age* (DTL, London, 1982).

Tournier, P., *Learning to Grow Old* (Highland, Crowborough, 1985 edition).

Virgo, L., *First Aid in Pastoral Care* chs. 1, 11. 12 (T. and T. Clark, Edinburgh, 1987).

Webber, A., *Growing into Fullness* (Marshall Pickering, Basingstoke, 1986).

Webber, A., *Life Later On* (Triangle, SPCK, London, 1990).

Other Grove publications which relate to this subject are:

Pastoral Series 43. *New Approaches to Ministry with Older People,* Arthur Creber, (September, 1990).

Spirituality Series 18. *Christians in Retirement,* Michael Botting.